D1475048

ON A STICK
COOKBOOK

50 Simple, Fun Recipes for the Campfire

by Julia Rutland

Adventure Publications
Cambridge, Minnesota

Cover and book design by Jonathan Norberg

Edited by Emily Beaumont

Illustrations by Emily Rutland unless otherwise noted

All images copyrighted.

Used under license from Shutterstock.com:
Cover image: **hugolascasse:** fire image

GraphicsRF: stick under recipe names; **Juliana Million:** page number
flame; **Lana_Samcorp:** hot dog on a stick under recipe names;
vectorisland: marshmallow on divider pages

10 9 8 7 6 5 4 3

On A Stick Cookbook: 50 Simple, Fun Recipes for the Campfire
Copyright © 2019 by Julia Rutland
Published by Adventure Publications
An imprint of AdventureKEEN
310 Garfield Street South
Cambridge, Minnesota 55008
(800) 678-7006
www.adventurepublications.net
All rights reserved
Printed in China
ISBN 978-1-59193-821-7 (pbk.); ISBN 978-1-59193-822-4 (ebook)

To my favorite camping companions, Dit, Emily, and Corinne

Table of Contents

ENTRÉES

APPETIZERS & SIDES

BREAKFAST

Cooking on a Stick

Campfire cooking purists use a slender branch to hold food over hot coals. This old-school method is charming and creates a fun activity as your family and friends search for the ideal cooking sticks. Choose a branch or stick long enough to reach the fire. The stick should be sturdy enough to hold food without breaking, yet slim enough that food can easily slide on. Green wood will be more resistant to catching fire than old, dry sticks. Whittle the end of the stick into a point with a pocket knife.

While branches are authentic, metal and wood skewers (see page 11) make campfire cooking easy and convenient.

Some recipes require a longer cooking time over the fire, and you may not want to hold a heavy skewer or stand near the heat for more than a few minutes. To give yourself a break, here are few techniques to try.

- Use very long skewers, and prop them up against the rocks that form the perimeter of the fire ring.

- Place skewers on a grill grate over the fire; turn as needed.

- Use long barbecue tongs to hold the skewer; this will lengthen the distance between your hand and the fire.

Tips for Campfire Cooking

Cooking over an open wood fire is the ultimate experience.

- Only make a campfire where it's allowed and always be aware of burn restrictions in your area, especially in areas where forest fires are a risk. If possible, use an established fire pit. If creating your own, look for a large, flat rock or a layer of sand as a base, making sure roots and leaves are well out of the way to prevent errant fires. Avoid overhanging branches. Pile rocks around the outside as a windbreak and to contain flames and sparks.

- Have firewood and lots of tinder (dry leaves, grass, wood shavings) and kindling (small twigs and branches) in piles ready to use. If gathering, look for dry wood that snaps easily. Try to use logs no larger than your wrist or forearm because large logs take a while to get started.

- Keep a bucket of water, fire extinguisher, or shovel for tossing sand and dirt to put out the fire. After you're done, scatter ashes and embers and sprinkle with water, stirring occasionally, until smoldering stops.

- If you're camping, be sure to familiarize yourself with bear safety tips before cooking at your campsite or storing food outdoors.

How to Build a Campfire

Tepee-style campfire

Arrange kindling in a cone shape around a small pile of tinder. Once lit, add logs a few at a time.

Log cabin-style campfire

Place two equal-size logs side by side, leaving a few inches in between. Add two logs on top, perpendicular to the first two, to form a square. Repeat for a few more layers, using the largest logs on the bottom. Leave space between logs so the fire can get oxygen. Place tinder in the center, and top with kindling and more tinder.

Pyramid-style campfire

Place four of the largest logs side by side. Place another layer on top, perpendicular to the first logs. Continue to alternate logs, using the smallest on top to form a pyramid shape. Place kindling and tinder on top.

Types of Skewers

Wood Skewers

Often made from bamboo, this inexpensive option comes in sizes from 6 to 12 inches. They must be soaked in water at least 30 minutes before cooking to avoid burning. Thin wood skewers should not be overloaded with food or the weight may cause them to snap. Use a barbecue mitt or oven mitt to protect your hands. Or place skewers on a greased grill rack over the coals.

Tip: Specialty campfire skewers are about 3 feet long and as thick as dowels. These can take more heat before burning up. For foods requiring more than 5 minutes of cooking time, soaking is recommended. Place skewers, pointed side down, in a tall beverage pitcher filled with water.

Tip: Short, round, or flat bamboo skewers are ideal for uncooked appetizers, but they aren't long enough to safely use around a campfire.

Metal Skewers

Strong in relation to their thickness, metal skewers are reusable and are sold in a variety of lengths. Twisted metal skewers are designed to hold food securely but can cause smaller fruits and vegetables to split apart. Metal skewers won't burn, but the handles can get hot, so use potholders or towels to protect hands from heat. This heat is useful, however, as it helps to cook dense vegetables and meat from the inside.

Making Biscuit Dough Cups

Called a Biscuit Cup Roaster, Wolf'em Stick, or Cobbler Stick, this gadget can create a cooked dough "cup" that can be used to hold savory or sweet fillings. When using refrigerated dough, regular-size biscuit dough is easier to shape into a cup than the triangular crescent roll dough. Extra-large biscuits will occasionally stay raw near the center. If the outside is done to the point of overcooking but the interior is raw, pull the dough cup off of the form and cook the inside of the cup over a grill grate. Or hold the dough cup over the heat with tongs or by skewering the top.

Keep refrigerated biscuit dough chilled as long as possible. If warm, the dough will stretch and tear around the form.

Cooking the biscuit cups can take up to 10 minutes, depending on the heat of the fire. That's a long time for hungry campers to wait, so prepare several at a time.

Cooking Techniques and Kebab Tips

Food cooks best over a bed of hot coals. For the hottest and most evenly cooked food, first allow the fire to burn until white-hot coals are visible. High, yellow flames will warm small foods, but they will only char the outside of dense foods.

Without a specialty thermometer, it's difficult to know the temperature of the campfire. Use the hand test to determine if fire and coals are hot enough to cook over. Hold your palm 3 to 4 inches above the heat. If you can only hold it for 1 to 2 seconds, that's high heat, which is good for searing meat but will probably burn other foods. If you can hold it for 4 to 5 seconds, that is medium, which is good for most foods; any longer is medium-low to low, good for warming cooked foods and breads.

Cut ingredients into equal-size pieces for even cooking. Other-wise, the small pieces may burn up before the larger pieces are done in the center.

Remember food safety. Keep meat and cut fruits and veggies chilled on ice before prep and cooking. To avoid cross contamination, cut meats on one side of the cutting board with fruits and veggies on the other, making sure the knife is washed or sanitized in between. Or cut fruits and vegetables first, and then cut meats. Once cooked, wrap leftovers after 2 hours and keep them iced or refrigerated.

Cook ground meats and poultry until they are completely done. As long as the outside of steaks are seared (the cut surfaces are where bacteria lurk), then it's okay to enjoy a medium-rare inside bite.

Space ingredients along skewers so that the heat can circulate around the pieces.

If ingredients spin on the skewer, food on the heavy side can overcook while the lighter side remains uncooked. To solve this problem, double up and use two parallel skewers per kebab.

For food that is too small to skewer or otherwise unruly, create a sling of aluminum foil between forked branches. Use the foil sling like a skillet over hot coals.

Sometimes food slips off sticks and skewers during cooking. If the coals in the fire are not hot enough, dough tends to "melt" and slither off before the heat can bake the dough into place. Avoid excessive use of oil or vegetable cooking spray.

Remember to clean up any leftover food scraps. It won't be unusual to lose a piece of food off the skewer every now and then. Allow dropped food to burn completely to later discourage critters from poking through the campfire for a midnight snack.

Helper Recipes

Store these in airtight containers in the refrigerator for up to 1 month.

Chocolate Sauce: Combine 1 cup heavy cream and ½ cup light corn syrup in a small saucepan over medium-low heat. Cook, stirring well, until hot. Remove from heat and stir in 8 ounces coarsely chopped sweet dark or semisweet chocolate. Let stand 5 minutes or until chocolate melts. Whisk until smooth.

Cinnamon-Sugar: Combine equal parts ground cinnamon and granulated sugar, stirring until well blended. Store in a small jar or airtight container up to 1 year.

Honey Mustard: Combine ½ cup Dijon mustard, 3 tablespoons mayonnaise, and 3 tablespoons honey in a small bowl. Serve with grilled chicken wings, chicken strips, pretzels, or as a sandwich spread.

Sriracha Mustard: Combine ½ cup yellow or Dijon mustard, 3 tablespoons Sriracha, and 1 tablespoon honey in a small bowl. Serve with warm pretzels, hot dogs, or sausages.

Hoisin Sauce: Combine ¼ cup soy sauce, 2 tablespoons peanut butter or bean paste, 2 tablespoons brown sugar, 1 tablespoon molasses, 1 teaspoon seasoned rice vinegar, 1 teaspoon sesame oil, and ½ teaspoon Chinese 5-spice seasoning in a small bowl. Season with Sriracha or hot sauce, to taste. Serve with grilled chicken, beef, tofu, or vegetables.

Teriyaki Sauce: Combine 3 tablespoons low-sodium soy sauce, ¼ cup brown sugar, ¼ teaspoon ground ginger, ¼ teaspoon garlic powder, and ⅛ teaspoon crushed red pepper flakes (optional) in a small saucepan over medium heat. Cook about 1 minute or until hot. Stir together ½ cup water and 1 tablespoon cornstarch in a small bowl until smooth. Stir into soy sauce mixture; cook 2 or 3 minutes or until thickened. Drizzle over grilled chicken, shrimp, steak, burgers, or vegetables.

Tzatziki Sauce: Combine 1 cup Greek yogurt; 1 tablespoon fresh lemon juice; ½ English cucumber, finely diced or shredded; 1 teaspoon dillweed; and 1 teaspoon salt in a bowl. Serve with grilled chicken, burgers, vegetables, and pita bread.

DESSERTS

Chocolate-Raspberry S'mores

What You Need

Graham cracker squares
Seedless raspberry jam or preserves
Dark or milk chocolate candy bars
Large marshmallows

Directions

Spread one side of half of the graham crackers with raspberry jam. Place a square of chocolate on top of jam.

For each s'more, skewer a marshmallow and cook until gooey and desired degree of doneness. Place marshmallow on top of chocolate; then top with a remaining graham cracker.

Chocolate Chip-Peanut Butter S'mores

What You Need

Chocolate chip cookies
Peanut butter, almond butter, or
  chocolate-hazelnut spread
Dark or milk chocolate candy bars
Large marshmallows

Directions

Spread flat side of half of the cookies with peanut butter. Place a square of chocolate on top of peanut butter.

For each s'more, skewer a marshmallow and cook until gooey and desired degree of doneness. Place marshmallow on top of chocolate; then top with a remaining cookie.

Lemon Meringue S'mores

What You Need

Vanilla wafers, shortbread, or
   gingersnap cookies
Lemon curd
Large marshmallows

Directions

Spread one side of half of the cookies with
lemon curd.

For each s'more, skewer a marshmallow
and cook until gooey and desired degree of
doneness. Place marshmallow on top of lemon
curd; then top with a remaining cookie.

Elvis S'mores

What You Need

Graham cracker squares
Peanut butter
Banana
Large marshmallows
Cooked bacon pieces

Directions

Spread one side of half of the graham crackers with peanut butter. Slice banana, and place 2 or 3 slices on top of peanut butter.

For each s'more, skewer a marshmallow and cook until gooey and desired degree of doneness. Place marshmallow on top of banana slices; top with bacon and a remaining graham cracker.

Fun-size Candy Bar Pockets

What You Need

Fun-size candy bars
Refrigerated crescent roll or biscuit dough

Directions

Place a candy bar in center of a triangle of
dough. Roll up, pinching sides to seal dough.

Place on a skewer. Cook until dough is golden
brown and inside is hot and melted.

Strawberry, Brownie, and Marshmallow Kebabs

What You Need

Fresh strawberries, hulled
Mini-brownie muffins
Large marshmallows
Chocolate syrup

Directions

Thread strawberries, mini-brownie muffins, and marshmallows on skewers.

Cook about 2 to 5 minutes, rotating skewers, until marshmallows are gooey and browned. Drizzle with syrup.

Strawberry and Pound Cake Dippers

What You Need

Chocolate Sauce (page 14 or store-bought)
   or chocolate-hazelnut spread
Kahlúa (optional)
Fresh strawberries, hulled
Pound cake, cut into 1-inch squares

Directions

Heat Chocolate Sauce in a pan of hot water
or in a metal bowl over the fire. If desired, stir
in Kahlúa.

Thread strawberries and pound cake onto
skewers. Dip in Chocolate Sauce.

Grilled Strawberry Shortcake Kebabs

What You Need

Fresh strawberries, hulled
Honey
Turbinado, coarse-grain sugar, or brown sugar
Cooked biscuits, cut into quarters
Sweetened whipped cream

Directions

Dip strawberries in honey, and roll in sugar.
Thread onto skewers with biscuit pieces.
Cook until sugar is bubbly and biscuits begin
to brown.

Dip into or spread with whipped
cream. Serve with additional
honey, if desired.

Banana and Chocolate-Hazelnut Mini Sandwiches

What You Need

Bananas
Brown sugar
Hawaiian sweet dinner rolls
Chocolate-hazelnut spread

Directions

Cut banana into large chunks and thread onto skewers. Roll in brown sugar.

Split rolls in half, and spread insides with chocolate-hazelnut spread.

Cook skewers, rotating occasionally, until golden brown and warm.

Place bananas in center of rolls.

Apple Pie on a Stick

What You Need

Small apples
Melted butter
Cinnamon-Sugar (page 15
  or store-bought)
Refrigerated crescent roll dough
Butterscotch chips

Directions

Core apples, cut into quarters, and thread onto long metal skewers. Cook, rotating slowly, until apple is hot and slightly soft. Dip apple skewers in melted butter, and roll in Cinnamon-Sugar.

Unroll dough and sprinkle butterscotch chips in center of each triangle. Place a skewered apple wedge on top; roll up dough around skewer. Cook until dough is done and golden brown.

Sweet-and-Salty Popcorn Balls

What You Need

Popped popcorn
Mini chocolate chips or mini candy-coated
  chocolate chips
Mini pretzels, slightly crushed
Large marshmallows

Directions

Mix together popcorn, chocolate chips, and
pretzels in a pie plate.

For each ball, thread a marshmallow onto a
skewer. Cook until soft and puffy.

Roll marshmallow in popcorn mixture.

Grilled Doughnuts and Berries with Chocolate Sauce

What You Need

Doughnut holes or doughnuts cut into pieces
Fresh strawberries, hulled
Blackberries
Chocolate Sauce (page 14 or store-bought)
Strawberry cream cheese

Directions

Thread doughnut holes and berries onto skewers.

Cook until warm.

Drizzle with or dip into Chocolate Sauce or spread with strawberry cream cheese.

Fudge Bites with Sea Salt Caramel

What You Need

Fudge cubes, chilled or frozen and just
  slightly thawed
Refrigerated crescent roll dough
Store-bought caramel sauce
Flaky sea salt

Directions

Thread fudge cubes onto skewers. Separate
crescent roll dough into triangles; cut each
triangle in half, and wrap dough around each
fudge piece, pressing to seal.

Cook skewers, rotating occasionally, until
dough is cooked and golden brown. Heat
caramel sauce in a pan of hot water or in a
metal bowl over the fire.

Dip skewers in caramel and sprinkle with salt.

Caramel-Berry Biscuit Cups

What You Need

Refrigerated biscuit dough
Canned sweetened whipped cream
Store-bought caramel sauce or chocolate syrup
Fresh strawberries (hulled), blackberries,
   raspberries, and/or blueberries

Directions

Flatten each biscuit dough piece into a disk,
and wrap around a metal grilling cup or 1½- to
2-inch-thick wood dowel or cooking branch.

Cook, rotating slowly, until biscuit
is golden brown and cooked through.
Pop off of form and place on a
plate. Squirt whipped cream into
bottom half and drizzle with
caramel sauce; top with berries.

Orange Brownie Cups

What You Need

6 navel or seedless oranges
1 package brownie mix
Orange juice (optional)

Directions

Cut about ⅓ off the top of each orange. Spoon out insides, placing orange pieces in a bowl.

Prepare brownie mix according to package directions, using orange juice in place of water, if desired. Stir in orange pieces. Spoon batter evenly into each hollowed-out orange, filling about ⅔ full. Replace orange tops on filled oranges; wrap with aluminum foil. Skewer each orange and cook over hot coals about 15 minutes or until done.

ENTRÉES

Tornado Dogs

What You Need

Hot dogs
Refrigerated crescent roll dough
Toppings: ketchup and mustard

Directions

Thread a hot dog onto each skewer. Cut hot dog around skewer, rotating to create a spiral cut. Gently spread hot dog apart to create space.

Separate crescent roll dough in triangles. Wind a dough triangle into the space around each hot dog, stretching dough to span the length of the hot dog.

Cook 8 to 10 minutes, rotating often, until hot dogs are hot and dough is golden brown. Dip in desired toppings.

BBQ Bacon-Chicken Kebabs

What You Need

Boneless, skinless chicken breasts
Thick-cut bacon
Store-bought barbecue sauce

Directions

Cut chicken breasts into long strips, about
½-inch wide.

Wrap 1 slice bacon around each chicken
strip. Weave onto a metal skewer.

Cook kebabs 10 minutes, rotating
occasionally. Brush with barbecue
sauce, and continue to cook about
5 minutes or until chicken is
completely done and bacon is
somewhat crispy. Serve with
additional sauce, if desired.

Grilled Pesto Chicken Kebabs

What You Need

Boneless, skinless chicken breasts
Cherry or grape tomatoes
Store-bought refrigerated pesto sauce

Directions

Cut chicken into bite-size pieces.

Thread chicken and tomatoes onto skewers.
Brush with pesto sauce.

Cook kebabs about 10 to 15 minutes, rotating occasionally, until chicken is completely cooked. Drizzle with additional pesto sauce, if desired.

Caribbean Chicken-and-Pineapple Kebabs

What You Need

Red bell pepper
Red onion
Boneless, skinless chicken breasts
Pineapple chunks
Vegetable oil
Caribbean Jerk seasoning

Directions

Cut bell pepper and onion into squares.
Cut chicken into bite-size pieces.

Thread chicken, bell pepper, onion, and
pineapple onto skewers. Brush with oil and
sprinkle with seasoning.

Cook kebabs about 10 to 15 minutes, rotating occasionally, until chicken is completely
cooked and vegetables are tender.

Sweet-and-Spicy Chicken

What You Need

Boneless, skinless chicken breasts
Apricot jelly
Smoked Tabasco Chipotle Pepper Sauce or
chipotle peppers

Directions

Cut chicken breasts into long strips, about 1½
inches wide.

Weave chicken strips onto skewers.

In a small bowl, combine about ¼ to ⅓ cup
apricot jelly with 1 tablespoon Tabasco or
chopped chipotle peppers. Brush over chicken;
cook 10 to 15 minutes or until chicken is completely done. Baste with apricot sauce while
chicken cooks.

Greek Chicken Kebabs

What You Need

Zucchini
Purple onion
Red bell pepper
Boneless, skinless chicken breasts
Olive oil
Lemon juice
Greek seasoning (dried oregano, salt, pepper)
Tzatziki Sauce (page 15 or store-bought)

Directions

Cut vegetables into 1-inch pieces. Cut chicken into bite-size pieces. Thread all onto skewers.

Stir together 2 parts oil and 1 part juice; brush over kebabs. Sprinkle with seasoning.

Cook 15 minutes, rotating occasionally, until chicken is done. Serve with Tzatziki Sauce.

Chicken Fajitas

What You Need

Red, yellow, or green bell pepper
Onion
Boneless, skinless chicken breasts
Taco seasoning mix
Flour tortillas
Lime wedges

Directions

Cut bell pepper and onion into 1-inch pieces. Cut chicken into bite-size pieces. Toss with seasoning mix. Thread all onto skewers.

Cook 15 minutes, rotating occasionally, until chicken is done. Place a skewer in the center of each tortilla; wrap tortilla around chicken and vegetables and pull the skewer away. Squeeze lime juice over top.

Honey-and-Lime Chicken Kebabs

What You Need

Boneless, skinless chicken breasts
Honey
Lime juice
Sriracha
Garlic salt

Directions

Cut chicken into bite-size pieces.

In a bowl, stir together equal parts honey and lime juice. Stir in Sriracha and garlic salt.

Thread chicken onto skewers. Coat chicken in sauce; cover and chill up to 2 hours.

Cook skewers, rotating occasionally, until chicken is completely done.

Grilled Chicken, Bacon, and Bread Kebabs

What You Need

Boneless, skinless chicken breasts
Thick-cut bacon
French bread
Cherry tomatoes
Store-bought Italian vinaigrette

Directions

Cut chicken into 1½-inch cubes. Slice bacon crosswise into 2-inch pieces. Cut bread into 1½-inch cubes.

Thread chicken, bacon, bread, and tomatoes onto skewers. Brush with vinaigrette.

Cook, rotating skewers, for 10 to 15 minutes or until chicken is completely done, bacon is crispy, and bread is golden brown.

Hoisin Pepper Beef Spirals

What You Need

Green onions
Flank or skirt steak
Cherry tomatoes
Hoisin Sauce (page 15 or store-bought)

Directions

Cut green onions into 1-inch pieces. Cut beef into 1- x 5-inch strips. Place a few green onion pieces and a cherry tomato on one end of each beef strip. Roll up and thread onto a skewer. Brush with Hoisin Sauce.

Cook 10 minutes, turning occasionally, or until meat reaches desired degree of doneness.

Note: It's okay to thread more than one spiral on a skewer if skewers are heavy-duty and won't bow under the weight of the food.

Meatball Sub on a Stick

What You Need

Prepared meatballs, thawed if frozen
Refrigerated pizza crust dough
Shredded Italian cheese blend
Store-bought marinara sauce

Directions

Thread 2 or 3 meatballs onto
metal skewers. Cook 5 minutes
or until warm.

Cut dough into squares (each large enough to
wrap around skewered meatballs). Sprinkle
cheese in center of each dough square, and
then wrap dough carefully around meatballs.

Cook skewers about 5 to 8 minutes, rotating
occasionally, until dough is cooked and golden
brown. Cool slightly; dip in marinara sauce.

Steakhouse Beef Kebabs

What You Need

Worcestershire sauce
Soy sauce
Olive oil
Dijon mustard
Garlic powder
Coarse-ground black pepper
Sirloin or other beef steak, cut into cubes
Red onion, cut into large pieces
Cremini or button mushrooms, stems removed

Directions

At home, combine first 3 ingredients in a bowl.
Stir in mustard, garlic powder, and pepper. Add
steak, onion, and mushrooms. Chill 8 hours.
Thread steak and vegetables onto skewers.

At campfire, cook until steak is done (8 minutes).

Cheesy Italian Sub

What You Need

Soft Italian bread
Store-bought Italian dressing
Sliced Swiss or Provolone cheese
Thinly sliced deli ham, salami, and smoked turkey
Sliced sweet onion
Shredded iceberg lettuce
Sliced tomato

Directions

Cut bread into 4-inch lengths. Split bread in half lengthwise. Drizzle with Italian dressing. Top with cheese, meat, onion, lettuce, and tomato. Drizzle with additional Italian dressing.

Wrap each sandwich in aluminum foil. Using two skewers side by side, skewer sandwich down the center. Cook, rotating, until hot.

Rosemary Pork-and-Orange Kebabs

What You Need

Pork tenderloin, cut into large cubes
Navel oranges, cut into wedges or slices
Soy sauce
Apricot preserves
Garlic powder or seasoning salt
Dried rosemary

Directions

Thread pork and oranges onto skewers. In a
small bowl, add soy sauce to apricot preserves
to thin. Stir in garlic powder and rosemary.
Brush mixture onto kebabs.

Cook skewers, rotating occasionally, until
pork is done.

Ham, Peach, and Maple Skewers

What You Need

½- to 1-inch-thick sliced ham
Fresh peaches
Maple syrup

Directions

Cut ham into cubes. Peel peaches, remove pits, and cut into thick wedges.

Thread ham and peaches onto skewers.

Cook skewers, rotating occasionally, until ham is heated and peaches are tender. Drizzle with maple syrup.

Gumbo on a Stick

What You Need

Smoked andouille sausage, sliced into pieces
Boneless, skinless chicken breasts, cut into
  bite-size pieces
Green bell pepper, cut into squares
Yellow or white onion, cut into squares
Cherry tomatoes
Olive or vegetable oil
Cajun or Creole seasoning blend
Cooked white rice

Directions

Thread sausage, chicken, bell pepper, onion,
and tomatoes onto skewers. Brush with oil
and sprinkle with seasoning blend.

Cook skewers 5 to 10 minutes, rotating occasionally, until chicken is done. Serve with rice.

Pepperoni Pizza Rolls

What You Need

Refrigerated French bread dough
Sliced pepperoni
Shredded mozzarella
Store-bought marinara sauce

Directions

Cut dough crosswise into 3-inch pieces, and
roll flat with a rolling pin. Layer pepperoni in
center of each dough piece, and top with
mozzarella. Roll edges of bread together,
and pinch to seal.

Zigzag pizza rolls onto soaked wood skewers.

Cook, rotating slowly, until bread is done and
insides are hot and melted.

Dip in warm marinara sauce.

APPETIZERS AND SIDES

Savory Salami S'mores

What You Need

Sliced salami or pepperoni
Large whole-grain crackers or
  melba toast rectangles
Provolone or Swiss cheese slices
Italian seasoning blend
Crushed red pepper flakes (optional)

Directions

Place salami slices on half of the crackers. Cut cheese into ½-inch-thick slices (half as wide as a cracker). Thread cheese onto skewers.

For each s'more, cook cheese, rotating skewer, until cheese is soft but not completely melted. Place cheese on top of salami; sprinkle with seasoning and, if desired, pepper flakes. Top with a remaining cracker.

Sausage-and-Pineapple Bites

What You Need

Cooked smoked sausage
Pineapple chunks
Teriyaki Sauce (page 15 or store-bought)

Directions

Cut sausage into 1-inch pieces. Thread sausage
and pineapple onto short skewers.

Brush with Teriyaki Sauce.

Note: To serve warm, thread sausage and
pineapple onto long skewers; cook 3 to
5 minutes or until sausage and pineapple
are warm and sauce is bubbly.

Bacon Pretzel Pups

What You Need

Frozen pretzel bites or soft pretzels (cut into
 1½- to 2-inch pieces), thawed
Coarse-ground mustard or honey mustard
Cocktail sausages
Precooked or raw bacon

Directions

Cut pretzel bites or pieces in half. Spread
cut sides with mustard. For each bite, top
1 pretzel half with 1 sausage; then top with
another pretzel half.

Cut bacon in half crosswise and wrap around
each pretzel. Thread several on a skewer,
leaving space in between.

Cook, rotating occasionally, until bacon is
crisp. Dip in additional mustard, if desired.

Sweet-and-Spicy Lil' Pigs

What You Need

Refrigerated crescent roll dough
Cream cheese
Pepper jelly
Cocktail sausages

Directions

Unroll crescent roll dough on a flat surface and separate into triangles. Cut each triangle in half, creating 2 triangles. Place a ½-inch cube of cream cheese and a small dollop of pepper jelly in the center of each triangle. Top with a cocktail sausage. Roll up and pinch dough together. Skewer through center of sausage.

Cook, rotating occasionally, until dough is golden brown and sausage is warm. Dip in additional pepper jelly, if desired.

Grilled Cheesy Corn

What You Need

Ears of fresh corn
Mayonnaise
Garlic salt
Chili powder or taco seasoning mix
Shredded Parmesan or Cheddar cheese

Directions

Shuck corn and remove silks. If desired, break ears in half. Pierce corn halfway into bottom with a metal skewer. Cook, rotating skewer, 10 to 15 minutes or until kernels are tender and golden brown.

Combine mayonnaise with garlic salt and chili powder. Spread mayonnaise mixture over corn. Cook until heated and bubbly. Sprinkle with cheese; cook until melted and bubbly.

Easy Seasoned Potatoes

What You Need

Yukon Gold or red potatoes
Olive oil
Seasoned salt or any seasoning blend

Directions

Cut potatoes into wedges. Thread potatoes
onto a skewer. Brush with oil and sprinkle
with seasoning.

Cook, rotating occasionally, until potatoes are
cooked through and golden brown. Sprinkle
with additional seasoning, if desired.

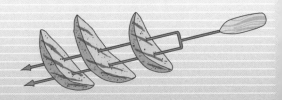

Garlic-Parmesan Potato Tornadoes

What You Need

Yukon Gold or red potatoes
Melted butter
Garlic salt
Grated Parmesan cheese

Directions

Push a metal skewer through center of potato. Cut potato at an angle around skewer, rotating potato, to create a spiral cut. Stretch potato along skewer.

Brush potato with melted butter. Sprinkle with garlic salt.

Cook 15 to 20 minutes, rotating and basting occasionally with additional melted butter, until potato is tender and golden brown. Sprinkle with cheese.

Cheesy Grilled Potatoes

What You Need

Yukon Gold or red potatoes
Mayonnaise
Dijon mustard
Grated Cheddar cheese

Directions

At home, cook potatoes in a microwave or boiling water for 5 minutes until almost cooked through. Cool slightly. Wrap in foil to transport.

At campfire, cut potatoes in half. Thread potatoes onto metal skewers. Stir together ¼ cup mayonnaise and 1 tablespoon mustard; brush mixture over potatoes.

Cook, rotating occasionally, until potatoes are hot and golden brown. Sprinkle with cheese. Cook until cheese is bubbly.

Ratatouille Kebabs

What You Need

Zucchini
Yellow squash
Red bell pepper
Onion
Cherry tomatoes
Mushrooms
Olive oil
Italian seasoning
Salt and pepper

Directions

Slice zucchini, squash, bell pepper, and onion
into ¼-inch-thick pieces. Thread with tomatoes
and mushrooms onto skewers. Brush with oil
and sprinkle with seasoning, salt, and pepper.

Cook until vegetables are hot and tender.

Canadian Bacon-Wrapped Shrimp

What You Need

Canadian bacon
Peeled and deveined cooked shrimp
Pineapple chunks
Hoisin Sauce (page 15 or store-bought)

Directions

Cut Canadian bacon in half. Place 1 shrimp
and 1 pineapple chunk in center, and thread
onto skewers.

Stir water into Hoisin Sauce to make a syrupy
glaze. Brush over skewers.

Cook, stirring occasionally, until golden
brown and edges of bacon are crisp.
Brush with additional Hoisin Sauce before
serving, if desired.

Veggie Hobo Packs

What You Need

Zucchini or yellow squash
Sweet onion
Cherry tomatoes, halved
Fresh spinach or kale
Olive oil or butter
Salt and pepper or seasoning salt

Directions

Cut aluminum foil into 15-inch pieces. Slice
squash and onion about ¼-inch thick. Place
with tomatoes in center of foil. Add spinach.
Drizzle with oil; sprinkle with salt and pepper.

Fold foil into a packet, pinching sides to seal.
Slide skewers through folded edges on two
sides. Cook 5 to 8 minutes or until package
sizzles and steam comes out of seams or holes.

Boursin-Bacon-Wrapped Mushrooms

What You Need

Button or cremini mushrooms
Boursin Gournay cheese or other spreadable
  cheese blend
Precooked bacon

Directions

Remove stems from mushrooms; spoon
Boursin into mushroom caps. Cut bacon slices
in half and wrap around mushrooms. Thread
several mushrooms onto a skewer, leaving at
least 1 inch in between.

Cook until bacon crisps, mushrooms become
tender, and cheese melts.

BREAKFAST

Sweet-and-Spicy Bacon Tots

What You Need

Precooked or raw bacon
Brown sugar
Chili powder
Ground cumin
Frozen tater tots, thawed

Directions

Cut bacon into thirds. Combine brown sugar and a bit of chili powder and ground cumin in a large zip-top plastic bag. Add bacon, tossing to coat.

Wrap bacon around tots, and thread onto a skewer with about ½- to 1-inch space in between.

Cook, rotating skewer, for 5 to 8 minutes or until bacon is crisp and tot is warm.

Waffle Breakfast Kebabs

What You Need

Mini-round waffles or traditional-size or
   Belgium-style waffles (cut into quarters)
Fresh strawberries, hulled
Bananas, cut into chunks
Blueberries
Maple syrup

Directions

Thread waffle pieces, strawberries, bananas,
and blueberries onto skewers.

Cook 5 to 8 minutes, turning occasionally,
until hot. Drizzle with maple syrup.

Bonus: Spread waffles with peanut butter
before threading onto skewers.

Banana-and-Granola Pops

What You Need

Granola
Slightly ripe bananas
Honey
Yogurt

Directions

Place granola in a large zip-top plastic bag and
crush lightly with a rolling pin. Peel bananas,
leaving whole, and skewer. Spread with honey
and roll in granola. Serve with yogurt.

Note: Be sure to use just-ripe bananas.
Overly ripe bananas won't remain on skewers.

Cinnamon Stick Biscuits

What You Need

Refrigerated biscuit dough
Melted butter
Cinnamon-Sugar (page 15 or store-bought)

Directions

Cut biscuits in half, and stretch each half into a long piece of dough. Wrap dough around a thick stick or twisted metal skewer.

Cook, rotating skewer, about 10 minutes or until dough is done and golden brown. Brush with melted butter and sprinkle with Cinnamon-Sugar.

Easy Cinnamon-Apple Bites

What You Need

Granny Smith or other tart apple
Refrigerated cinnamon roll dough with icing

Directions

Core apple and slice into 8 wedges. Cut
each cinnamon roll dough piece in half,
flatten slightly, and wrap each half around
an apple wedge. Thread wrapped apple
wedges onto skewers.

Cook, rotating skewers, until dough is done
and light golden brown. Drizzle with icing.

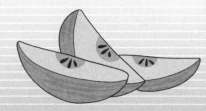

Breakfast Orange Cups

What You Need

Navel or seedless oranges
Eggs or egg substitute
Salt and pepper
Shredded Cheddar cheese
Cooked and crumbled bacon

Directions

Cut each orange in half and scoop out insides.
Crack or pour egg into orange. Sprinkle
with salt and pepper. Sprinkle with cheese
and bacon.

Skewer orange about ¼ inch from edge with
a long skewer. Cook 10 to 12 minutes or until
eggs are set.

Sausage-and-Gravy Biscuit Cups

What You Need

Refrigerated biscuit dough
Breakfast sausage
Prepared gravy or gravy mix

Directions

Flatten each piece of biscuit dough into a disk; wrap around a metal grilling cup or 1½- to 2-inch-thick wood dowel or branch.

Cook, rotating slowly, until biscuit is golden brown and cooked through. Pop off form and set aside.

Cook sausage in a skillet until browned and crumbly; drain. Heat prepared gravy, or prepare mix according to package directions. Spoon sausage into cups and top with gravy.

Egg-and-Sausage Kebabs

What You Need

Eggs
Salt and pepper
Vegetable oil
Cooked breakfast sausage patties, halved
Pancakes or English muffins, quartered
Maple syrup, warmed

Directions

At home, whisk 3 eggs in a bowl; add salt and
pepper. Heat oil in a nonstick skillet. Cook eggs
in a flat layer until done. Cool; roll into a cylin-
der. Cover with plastic wrap and refrigerate.

At campfire, cut eggs into 2-inch spirals.
Thread spirals, sausage, and pancakes onto
skewers. Cook until heated. Drizzle with
syrup, if desired.

About the Author

Julia Rutland is a Washington, D.C.-area food writer and recipe developer whose work appears regularly in publications and websites such as Weight Watchers books, *Southern Living* magazine, *Coastal Living* magazine, Myfitnesspal.com, and more. She is the coauthor of *Discover Dinnertime* and a contributor to many other cookbooks and websites.

Julia has visited all 50 states and camped with her family in most of them, sleeping in tents, campers, or occasionally just under the stars. Her kitchen gear takes up more space than the tent or other camping supplies because she feels that cooking outside is more fun than hiking. Julia lives in Purcellville, Virginia, with her husband, two daughters, a cat, a couple of dogs, too many chickens, and whatever animals decide to adopt them.

Visit Julia online at www.juliarutland.com